Neural-Symbolic AI

The Future of Explainable and Efficient AI

Introduction

Neural-Symbolic AI represents a groundbreaking fusion of two historically separate fields: deep learning (neural networks) and symbolic reasoning. By integrating these two approaches, Neural-Symbolic AI seeks to create intelligent systems that not only learn from data but also reason, interpret, and generalize beyond their training experience. This synergy offers a powerful alternative to purely statistical machine learning models, making AI systems more interpretable, flexible, and capable of logical reasoning.

In this comprehensive guide, we will explore the principles, advantages, and applications of Neural-Symbolic AI. Whether you're a beginner eager to understand the foundations or an AI expert looking to implement these techniques, this book will provide you with the necessary insights and tools to harness the power of this hybrid approach.

What You Will Learn

- The fundamentals of Neural-Symbolic AI, including key concepts and historical background
- Why combining symbolic reasoning with deep learning is crucial for the next generation of AI
- Real-world applications of Neural-Symbolic AI across various industries
- Step-by-step implementation techniques and frameworks
- Challenges, limitations, and future trends shaping the field of Neural-Symbolic AI

Chapter 1: The Foundations of Neural-Symbolic AI

1.1 Understanding Neural Networks and Symbolic AI

To appreciate the importance of Neural-Symbolic AI, we must first understand its two primary components: neural networks and symbolic reasoning.

1.1.1 Neural Networks

Neural networks, inspired by the human brain, are computational models designed to recognize patterns and make predictions from data. These models consist of interconnected layers of artificial neurons that learn representations from large datasets. They have revolutionized AI in fields such as computer vision, natural language processing (NLP), and reinforcement learning.

1.1.2 Symbolic AI

Symbolic AI, also known as Good Old-Fashioned AI (GOFAI), relies on predefined rules, logic, and knowledge representation to perform reasoning tasks. It enables machines to manipulate symbols, use logical inference, and follow structured problem-solving approaches. Unlike deep learning, symbolic AI is inherently interpretable and can explain its decision-making process.

1.2 Why Combine Neural Networks and Symbolic AI?

Although neural networks excel in learning from data, they often struggle with reasoning, generalization, and interpretability. Conversely, symbolic AI can reason effectively but lacks the flexibility and scalability of deep learning. By integrating these approaches, Neural-Symbolic AI aims to:

- Improve interpretability and trustworthiness of AI models

- Enhance generalization capabilities beyond training data
- Enable AI systems to learn and reason with structured knowledge
- Solve complex problems requiring both perception and logical reasoning

1.3 Historical Evolution of Neural-Symbolic AI

Neural-Symbolic AI is not a new concept. Research in this area dates back to the early days of AI but gained renewed interest with the rise of deep learning. Key milestones include:

- **1950s-1980s:** Early attempts at combining neural networks and rule-based AI
- **1990s-2000s:** Development of hybrid AI models for reasoning tasks
- **2010s-Present:** Advances in deep learning lead to renewed interest in integrating symbolic reasoning with neural networks

1.4 Key Techniques in Neural-Symbolic AI

Several methods have emerged to bridge the gap between neural and symbolic AI:

- **Neural-Symbolic Integration:** Embedding logic-based reasoning within deep learning frameworks
- **Knowledge Graphs and Deep Learning:** Using structured knowledge to enhance neural models
- **Hybrid AI Architectures:** Combining symbolic logic engines with neural networks
- **Rule-Based Augmentation:** Incorporating logical rules into neural network training

1.5 Summary

Neural-Symbolic AI offers a powerful approach to building more capable and interpretable AI systems. By merging the strengths of neural networks and symbolic reasoning, it paves the way for AI that can learn, reason, and generalize effectively. In the following chapters, we will delve deeper into its real-world applications, implementation strategies, and future potential.

Chapter 2: Key Components of Neural-Symbolic AI

2.1 Symbolic Reasoning

Symbolic reasoning is the foundation of traditional artificial intelligence, relying on explicit rules and logic to process information. It enables AI systems to perform logical inference, handle structured data, and operate with high interpretability.

Logic-based AI

Logic-based AI utilizes formal logic to encode knowledge and derive conclusions. Classical approaches include:

- **Propositional Logic**: Boolean logic statements used in simple rule-based AI.
- **First-Order Logic (FOL)**: More expressive than propositional logic, allowing the representation of objects, relations, and quantifiers.

- **Non-Monotonic Logic**: Handles reasoning with incomplete or evolving information.
- **Description Logics**: Used in ontologies for semantic reasoning.

Knowledge Representation

Knowledge representation involves structuring information so that AI can process it effectively. Common methods include:

- **Semantic Networks**: Graph-based structures where nodes represent concepts and edges denote relationships.
- **Frames and Scripts**: Encapsulated data structures storing stereotypical knowledge.
- **Ontologies**: Hierarchical frameworks defining concepts and relationships, widely used in expert systems and semantic web applications.

Rule-based Systems

Rule-based AI systems use **if-then** logic to model expert knowledge. Components include:

- **Production Rules**: Predefined conditions triggering specific actions.
- **Inference Engines**: Mechanisms for applying rules to draw conclusions.
- **Expert Systems**: AI applications using rule-based reasoning, such as MYCIN and DENDRAL.

2.2 Neural Networks

Neural networks are statistical models inspired by biological neurons. They are crucial for learning patterns in data and approximating functions.

Deep Learning Fundamentals

Deep learning involves training multi-layered neural networks to recognize complex patterns. Key aspects include:

- **Backpropagation**: Algorithm for adjusting weights based on error gradients.
- **Activation Functions**: Sigmoid, ReLU, and softmax used to introduce non-linearity.

- **Optimization Algorithms**: Stochastic Gradient Descent (SGD), Adam, and RMSprop for efficient learning.

Representation Learning

Neural networks automatically learn feature representations from raw data. This process enables:

- **Feature Extraction**: Learning abstract representations without explicit feature engineering.
- **Transfer Learning**: Adapting pre-trained models to new tasks.
- **Self-Supervised Learning**: Learning useful features without labeled data.

Connectionist Architectures

Various architectures power modern AI applications:

- **Convolutional Neural Networks (CNNs)**: Used in image processing.

- **Recurrent Neural Networks (RNNs)**: Suitable for sequential data.

- **Transformer Models**: State-of-the-art in natural language processing (NLP).

- **Autoencoders**: Used for dimensionality reduction and anomaly detection.

2.3 Hybrid Models

Hybrid models combine the strengths of symbolic reasoning and neural networks to create AI systems that are both interpretable and capable of learning from data.

Embedding Symbolic Reasoning into Neural Networks

By incorporating logical constraints into neural models, hybrid AI systems can:

- **Enhance Interpretability**: Providing explainable reasoning paths.

- **Improve Generalization**: Leveraging structured knowledge to reduce reliance on extensive training data.
- **Enable Robustness**: Reducing errors through symbolic guidance.

Neural Networks Augmenting Symbolic AI

Neural networks can enhance symbolic AI by:

- **Automating Knowledge Extraction**: Learning rules and relationships from unstructured data.
- **Handling Uncertainty**: Providing probabilistic reasoning mechanisms.
- **Scaling Up Reasoning**: Enabling symbolic AI to process vast datasets.

Probabilistic Logic Networks

Probabilistic Logic Networks (PLNs) are a crucial component of hybrid AI, integrating logic-based reasoning with probabilistic methods to manage uncertainty in decision-making.

Overview

PLNs extend classical logic by incorporating probability theory, enabling AI to reason under uncertainty. They use:

- **Bayesian Networks**: Graphical models representing probabilistic relationships.
- **Markov Logic Networks**: Combining first-order logic with probabilistic graphical models.
- **Stochastic Inference**: Approximating reasoning when exact computations are infeasible.

Key Components

PLNs consist of:

- **Probabilistic Rules**: Logical statements with associated probabilities.
- **Belief Networks**: Structures encoding dependencies among variables.

- **Uncertain Inference Mechanisms**: Algorithms for updating probabilities based on evidence.

Applications

PLNs have broad applications, including:

- **Medical Diagnosis**: AI-assisted systems reasoning under incomplete patient data.
- **Robotics**: Navigating dynamic environments with probabilistic planning.
- **Natural Language Processing**: Understanding ambiguous linguistic structures.

Advantages and Challenges

PLNs balance the structure of symbolic reasoning with the flexibility of probabilistic learning. However, they face challenges such as:

- **Computational Complexity**: Probabilistic inference can be computationally expensive.

- **Data Requirements**: Learning accurate probability distributions often requires large datasets.
- **Hybrid Integration**: Seamlessly merging symbolic and neural representations remains an active research area.

By leveraging PLNs, neural-symbolic AI can achieve both **explainability** and **robust learning**, making them a promising avenue for next-generation intelligent systems.

Chapter 3: Real-World Applications

Artificial Intelligence (AI) has evolved into a transformative force across industries, impacting sectors such as healthcare, finance, autonomous systems, and natural language processing (NLP). However, as AI continues to integrate into daily operations, explainability and interpretability have become critical factors for trust, reliability, and compliance. This chapter explores real-world applications where explainable AI (XAI), reasoning-based decision-making, and logical constraints play a crucial role in enhancing AI systems.

3.1 Healthcare

Medical Diagnosis with Explainable AI

One of the most significant applications of AI in healthcare is medical diagnosis. AI-powered diagnostic tools assist doctors in detecting diseases, analyzing medical images, and identifying patterns in patient data. However, black-box models often limit trust in these AI systems, making explainability essential.

Explainable AI provides transparent decision-making in diagnosis by using interpretable models such as decision trees, rule-based systems, and attention mechanisms in deep learning. For instance, in radiology, AI models analyzing X-rays and MRIs can highlight key image areas contributing to a diagnosis. Tools like LIME (Local Interpretable Model-Agnostic Explanations) and SHAP (Shapley Additive Explanations) help in visualizing the decision-making process of deep learning models, ensuring clinicians understand and trust AI-assisted decisions.

Drug Discovery Combining Reasoning and Learning

AI accelerates drug discovery by predicting molecular interactions, identifying potential drug candidates, and optimizing clinical trial processes. Hybrid AI models that combine machine learning and symbolic reasoning improve drug development efficiency. Knowledge graphs play a crucial role in reasoning about chemical compounds, biological interactions, and disease mechanisms, leading to more effective drug candidate selection.

For example, IBM's Watson for Drug Discovery integrates AI reasoning and learning to analyze biomedical literature, patent databases, and genomic datasets, helping researchers uncover hidden connections between molecules and diseases. Such explainable approaches ensure that scientists understand why a particular compound is suggested for further testing.

3.2 Finance

Fraud Detection with Interpretable Models

Fraud detection relies on AI models to analyze transaction patterns, identify anomalies, and prevent financial crimes. Traditional machine learning models detect fraud but often function as black boxes, making it difficult to justify flagged transactions. Interpretable models, such as decision trees, Bayesian networks, and rule-based systems, enhance transparency in fraud detection.

Financial institutions increasingly use explainable AI approaches, such as feature importance analysis, to show which transaction characteristics contribute to fraudulent behavior. For instance, an AI system may flag a transaction based on sudden changes in spending behavior, geolocation inconsistencies, or unusual merchant categories, with explanations provided to compliance officers.

Automated Trading Systems with Rule-Based Reasoning

Automated trading, or algorithmic trading, uses AI to execute financial transactions based on pre-defined rules and real-time data analysis. While deep learning models predict market trends, rule-based reasoning enhances decision-making by incorporating logical constraints and market regulations.

Hybrid AI trading systems combine machine learning for pattern recognition with symbolic AI for reasoning about economic indicators, ensuring more transparent and risk-aware trading strategies. These systems provide human traders with insights into why a particular stock is recommended for purchase or sale, improving confidence in AI-assisted investment strategies.

3.3 Autonomous Systems

Self-Driving Cars Leveraging Logical Constraints

Autonomous vehicles (AVs) rely on AI to perceive environments, make driving decisions, and navigate safely. However, deep learning models used in perception tasks, such as object detection and lane recognition, often lack interpretability. Incorporating logical constraints improves decision-making transparency in AVs.

Explainable AI techniques, such as probabilistic graphical models and constraint satisfaction algorithms, allow self-driving cars to justify route choices, braking decisions, and obstacle avoidance strategies. Companies like Waymo and Tesla use hybrid AI approaches, combining neural networks with rule-based reasoning to enhance reliability in unpredictable road scenarios.

Robotics with Reasoning-Based Decision-Making

AI-powered robots operate in various domains, from industrial automation to service robotics. Robots making autonomous decisions require explainability, particularly in high-risk environments such as manufacturing or healthcare.

Reasoning-based AI enables robots to explain their actions using symbolic logic and probabilistic reasoning. For example, in medical robotics, AI-assisted surgical robots can provide justifications for incision paths based on anatomical constraints and past surgical outcomes. In industrial settings, collaborative robots (cobots) use interpretable reinforcement learning to adapt to dynamic environments while ensuring safety for human coworkers.

3.4 Natural Language Processing (NLP)

Explainable Chatbots

Conversational AI systems, such as chatbots and virtual assistants, enhance customer service, healthcare support, and business automation. However, users often struggle to understand why chatbots provide certain responses, leading to trust issues. Explainable NLP models address this challenge by incorporating reasoning mechanisms.

Explainable chatbots use techniques such as attention visualization, rule-based dialogue generation, and knowledge graphs to provide users with transparent responses. For instance, a customer service chatbot can explain why it recommends a specific troubleshooting step based on past user interactions and documented solutions. In legal and healthcare domains, XAI-powered chatbots ensure compliance by justifying responses with relevant policies and medical guidelines.

Semantic Understanding in Search Engines

Search engines leverage NLP to retrieve and rank relevant content based on user queries. Traditional deep learning models for search ranking function as black boxes, making it difficult to understand why certain results appear at the top. Explainable AI enhances search engine transparency by incorporating semantic understanding techniques.

AI-powered search engines use interpretable embeddings, knowledge graphs, and semantic similarity measures to refine search results. For example, Google's BERT (Bidirectional Encoder Representations from Transformers) improves search relevance by understanding query context, while XAI tools explain how specific keywords influence ranking. Businesses using AI-driven search optimization benefit from interpretable algorithms that clarify how content matches user intent.

This chapter highlights the increasing need for explainability in AI applications across healthcare, finance, autonomous systems, and NLP. As AI adoption grows, integrating reasoning-based decision-making and interpretable models ensures that AI systems remain transparent, accountable, and trustworthy in real-world scenarios.

Chapter 4: Implementing Neural-Symbolic AI

4.1 Frameworks and Tools

Implementing Neural-Symbolic AI requires a combination of tools that cater to both symbolic reasoning and neural learning. Below are some key frameworks and tools that help integrate these paradigms effectively:

TensorFlow/Keras for Neural Networks

TensorFlow and Keras are widely used frameworks for developing neural networks. They provide robust libraries for deep learning, enabling training, optimization, and inference of neural models. Key features include:

- **Scalability**: Can handle large-scale machine learning tasks.
- **Pretrained Models**: Includes models like BERT, ResNet, and GPT for various applications.

- **Flexibility**: Supports custom model creation for hybrid AI systems.

Prolog and Logic-Based AI Tools

Prolog is a declarative programming language that specializes in symbolic reasoning, rule-based inference, and logical deductions. Other logic-based AI tools include:

- **DLV System**: For disjunctive logic programming.
- **Answer Set Programming (ASP)**: Useful for knowledge representation.
- **SWI-Prolog**: Provides built-in inference mechanisms for symbolic reasoning.

Knowledge Graphs for Structured Data

Knowledge graphs represent structured relationships among entities. They enhance symbolic reasoning by allowing logical queries over interconnected data. Popular tools include:

- **Neo4j**: A graph database supporting complex queries.

- **RDF/OWL**: Semantic web standards for knowledge representation.
- **SPARQL**: A query language for semantic graphs.

4.2 Step-by-Step Implementation

1. Define the Problem and Data

Before implementing a Neural-Symbolic AI model, clearly define the problem domain and identify the data required. This involves:

- Collecting structured (knowledge graphs, databases) and unstructured data (text, images).
- Defining symbolic rules and constraints relevant to the problem.
- Preparing datasets for training neural networks.

2. Build the Symbolic Knowledge Base

A symbolic knowledge base consists of explicitly defined rules and facts. Key steps:

- Use Prolog or ASP to define logical rules.
- Construct ontologies using RDF/OWL for structured representation.
- Develop a knowledge graph that connects different entities and relationships.

3. Train Neural Networks for Pattern Recognition

Neural networks learn patterns from raw data. The training process involves:

- Selecting an appropriate architecture (CNNs for images, RNNs for sequences, Transformers for NLP).
- Preprocessing data and augmenting training samples.
- Training the model using TensorFlow/Keras and optimizing hyperparameters.
- Evaluating performance using accuracy, precision, and recall.

4. Integrate Symbolic Reasoning with Neural Learning

Integration can be achieved using various techniques:

- **Neuro-Symbolic Embedding**: Convert symbolic representations into neural-compatible formats.
- **Hybrid Models**: Use a neural network to extract features, then apply symbolic reasoning for decision-making.
- **Knowledge Injection**: Pretrain neural networks with symbolic rules to guide learning.

5. Test and Refine the Model

Once the model is trained and integrated:

- Test the system against benchmark datasets.
- Analyze errors and refine symbolic rules or neural architectures.

- Optimize inference speed and accuracy by tuning model parameters.

4.3 Case Study: Building a Neural-Symbolic AI Model

To demonstrate the implementation process, let's build a simple Neural-Symbolic AI system for medical diagnosis. The system will:

- Use a **knowledge graph** to represent medical conditions, symptoms, and treatments.
- Employ **Prolog** for logical inference based on symptom-checking.
- Train a **neural network** to recognize symptoms from patient data.
- Integrate both approaches for accurate diagnosis.

Step 1: Define the Problem and Data

- Collect medical records containing symptoms and diagnoses.

- Build a knowledge graph linking symptoms to diseases.
- Use a dataset of medical images to train a neural network for symptom detection.

Step 2: Build the Symbolic Knowledge Base

```
has_symptom(john, fever).
has_symptom(john, cough).
diagnose(X, flu) :- has_symptom(X, fever),
has_symptom(X, cough).
```

This Prolog rule states that if a patient has both fever and cough, they may have the flu.

Step 3: Train a Neural Network for Symptom Detection

```
import tensorflow as tf
from tensorflow import keras

model = keras.Sequential([
    keras.layers.Dense(64, activation='relu',
input_shape=(num_features,)),
    keras.layers.Dense(32, activation='relu'),
```

```
    keras.layers.Dense(num_classes,
activation='softmax')
])

model.compile(optimizer='adam',
loss='categorical_crossentropy',
metrics=['accuracy'])
model.fit(train_data, train_labels, epochs=10,
validation_data=(test_data, test_labels))
```

This model classifies symptoms from patient data.

Step 4: Integrate Symbolic Reasoning with Neural Learning

Once the neural network predicts symptoms, it passes them to the Prolog-based inference engine for diagnosis.

```
import pyswip
prolog = pyswip.Prolog()
prolog.consult("medical_rules.pl")

symptoms_detected = ['fever', 'cough']
query = "diagnose(john, Disease)"
```

```
diagnosis = list(prolog.query(query))
print(diagnosis)
```

Step 5: Test and Refine the Model

- Evaluate diagnosis accuracy by comparing AI predictions with expert medical opinions.
- Adjust Prolog rules and neural network hyperparameters based on test results.
- Optimize the pipeline for real-time inference.

Conclusion

By combining neural networks and symbolic AI, we achieve a robust medical diagnosis system. This hybrid approach ensures:

- **Better Interpretability**: Symbolic rules provide human-readable explanations.
- **Improved Accuracy**: Neural networks enhance pattern recognition.
- **Scalability**: The system can adapt to new medical knowledge over time.

This case study illustrates the power of Neural-Symbolic AI in practical applications. Future improvements may include reinforcement learning for adaptive reasoning and graph neural networks for dynamic knowledge representation.

Chapter 5: Challenges and Future of Neural-Symbolic AI

5.1 Key Challenges

Neural-Symbolic AI combines the strengths of symbolic reasoning with neural networks, offering a hybrid approach to artificial intelligence. However, several challenges hinder its seamless implementation and adoption. Below are some of the most pressing issues:

Integration Complexity

Neural-Symbolic AI aims to merge two fundamentally different paradigms—symbolic AI, which relies on logic and rules, and neural networks, which learn from data-driven approaches. Integrating these two approaches is inherently complex due to the following factors:

- **Incompatibility of Representations**: Symbolic AI works with structured representations, such as knowledge graphs and logical rules, while neural networks rely on distributed representations that are harder to interpret.

- **Lack of Standardized Frameworks**: There is no universal approach for integrating symbolic logic with deep learning models, leading to inconsistencies in implementation.
- **Training Challenges**: Hybrid models must be trained efficiently without sacrificing the explainability and accuracy of the results, which requires sophisticated optimization techniques.

Computational Efficiency

Hybrid AI systems often require significant computational resources due to their dual nature. The key concerns include:

- **Resource Consumption**: Combining neural and symbolic reasoning demands more processing power and memory, potentially limiting scalability.
- **Inference Speed**: While deep learning models can process information quickly,

symbolic reasoning is often slower and may introduce latency.

- **Optimization Trade-offs**: Finding the right balance between efficiency, interpretability, and generalization remains an ongoing challenge.

Data Representation Bottlenecks

Effective data representation is crucial for bridging the gap between neural networks and symbolic reasoning. However, several issues arise:

- **Lack of Common Data Formats**: Symbolic reasoning requires structured data, while neural networks can work with unstructured data, making representation a bottleneck.
- **Knowledge Injection**: Incorporating symbolic knowledge into neural networks requires efficient encoding mechanisms, which are still under research.
- **Scalability Issues**: As the complexity of real-world problems grows, representing

vast amounts of knowledge in a structured yet efficient manner becomes increasingly difficult.

5.2 The Future of Hybrid AI

Despite these challenges, Neural-Symbolic AI holds great promise for the future. Ongoing research and technological advancements are addressing these limitations and paving the way for more efficient and interpretable AI systems.

Advances in Neuro-Symbolic Architectures

Several advancements are making it easier to integrate neural and symbolic approaches:

- **Differentiable Reasoning**: New architectures allow symbolic reasoning to be differentiable, making it possible to integrate logical reasoning within deep learning models.
- **Graph Neural Networks (GNNs)**: These networks provide a structured way to represent symbolic relationships, bridging

the gap between structured and unstructured data.

- **Hybrid Learning Paradigms**: Techniques such as reinforcement learning combined with symbolic reasoning enhance AI's decision-making capabilities in complex environments.

AI Ethics and Responsible AI

As AI systems become more powerful, ethical considerations become paramount. Neuro-symbolic AI offers opportunities to enhance AI's transparency and accountability:

- **Explainability**: Hybrid AI systems can provide human-readable explanations for their decisions, helping to build trust.
- **Fairness and Bias Mitigation**: Symbolic reasoning can help enforce fairness constraints and reduce bias in AI models.
- **Regulatory Compliance**: As AI regulations tighten, neuro-symbolic approaches can help ensure compliance by maintaining interpretable decision-making processes.

Emerging Research Trends

Research in Neural-Symbolic AI is expanding rapidly, with several promising directions:

- **Automated Knowledge Integration**: Developing methods to automatically extract and incorporate symbolic knowledge from large-scale datasets.
- **Neuromorphic Computing**: Exploring hardware solutions inspired by the human brain to enhance the efficiency of hybrid AI models.
- **Self-Learning AI Systems**: Enabling AI to continuously learn from both structured and unstructured data without extensive human intervention.

Neural-Symbolic AI is an evolving field with immense potential. While integration, efficiency, and data representation remain significant challenges, ongoing advancements in hybrid architectures, ethical AI, and emerging research trends promise a future where AI is both powerful and interpretable. As research progresses, we can expect neuro-symbolic AI to play a crucial role in building the next generation of intelligent systems.

Conclusion

Neural-Symbolic AI represents a groundbreaking paradigm in artificial intelligence, merging the strengths of neural networks with symbolic reasoning to create more robust, explainable, and efficient AI models. By integrating data-driven learning with logical inference, this hybrid approach offers superior generalization, enhanced interpretability, and the ability to handle complex reasoning tasks that traditional AI systems struggle with.

As AI continues to evolve, Neural-Symbolic AI is poised to play a crucial role in bridging the gap between deep learning and human-like reasoning. Whether you're a researcher, developer, or AI enthusiast, staying informed and implementing these hybrid techniques will keep you at the forefront of this transformative field.

Additional Resources

For those looking to deepen their understanding of Neural-Symbolic AI, the following resources provide valuable insights and hands-on experience:

- **Research Papers & Further Readings**
  - "Neural-Symbolic Learning and Reasoning" – Garcez et al.
  - "The Role of Symbolic Reasoning in Deep Learning" – Marcus & Davis
  - Various publications from conferences such as NeurIPS, ICML, and AAAI
- **Open-Source Projects**
  - IBM's Neuro-Symbolic AI initiatives
  - DeepMind's efforts in integrating logic with deep learning
  - Open-source tools like TensorFlow and PyTorch implementations
- **Online Courses & Tutorials**
  - Coursera and Udacity courses on Hybrid AI

- MIT and Stanford lectures on Explainable AI
- GitHub repositories with practical implementations

www.ingramcontent.com/pod-product-compliance
Lightning Source LLC
LaVergne TN
LVHW051751050326
832903LV00029B/2856